# LIVERPOOL to NORTH WALES PLEASURE-STEAMERS

## A Pictorial History 1821-1962

John Cowell

S.B. Publications
1990

First published in 1990 by S.B. Publications

5 Queen Margaret's Road, Loggerheads, Nr. Market Drayton, Shropshire TF9 4EP



British Library Cataloguing in Publication Data

Typeset, printed and bound by Manchester Free Press, Paragon Mill, Jersey Street, Manchester M4 6FP. Tel: 061-236 8822.

ISBN 1 870708 35 0

# CONTENTS



## ILLUSTRATIONS

# ILLUSTRATIONS

# ILLUSTRATIONS



Cover illustration: *St Tudno* (II), 1891-1912, Liverpool & North Wales Steamship Company.

# PREFACE

Pleasure-steamers will be remembered with affection by thousands of Merseyside and North Wales people, and this book attempts to recapture the nostalgic era of leisurely travel, now long since vanished. Most of the illustrations in the book are taken from picture postcards, particularly from the period 1902 to 1914. This was the golden age of postcards when they were sold everywhere, including aboard the steamers. They were sent by young and old, rich and poor, and by 1914 over 800 million cards were posted annually. This led to the great craze for collecting, thus preserving a marvellous record of life in Edwardian Britain before the widespread use of the box camera. Fortunately, shipping was a popular theme among postcard publishers so most of the pleasure-steamers were photographed; otherwise a visual record of some of them might have disappeared for ever.

Most of the postcards and photographs reproduced here are from the author's collection, compiled over a period of 20 years, some of which were originally in a collection carefully preserved by the Hughes family of Menai Bridge. John Gray Hughes succeeded his father as Piermaster in 1908 and during his 54 years in office he could boast that he had never once failed to meet the Liverpool steamers. When he retired in 1962 he was followed by his son Dennis, who sadly died in 1983, but not before he had helped to complete over a hundred years of unbroken family service on the pier. A few illustrations have also been taken from the postcard collection of the late John Brown, and I am grateful to Pam Brown for allowing me to use them.

Much of the detailed information on the vessels themselves has been obtained from F.C. Thornley's excellent book, *Steamers of North Wales*, and I am deeply indebted to the publishers, T. Stephenson & Sons Limited of Prescot, for kindly allowing me to draw on this book.

I acknowledge with gratitude the courteous help received from the Archivists and staff of the County Record Offices at Caernarfon and Llangefni, as well as at the University College of North Wales, Bangor. I have also received generous help from Peter Woolley and Peter Brindley, two enthusiastic postcard collectors, to whom I am most grateful.

# LIVERPOOL TO NORTH WALES PLEASURE-STEAMERS

A regular packet service between Liverpool and North Wales was established as early as 1821. On the 10th May the *North Wales Gazette* announced that the steam packet *Cambria* would be sailing to Bagillt, and informed readers that she was "fitted with every comfort and convenience, with accommodation for horses and carriages". The *Cambria* was launched two weeks later and made her first passage to Bagillt on the 4th June. The following year the service was extended to the Menai Straits by the newly-built *Albion*, and when she landed at Beaumaris on the 8th June with 35 passengers aboard she was greeted with cannonades and enthusiastic cheering. The *North Wales Gazette* carried a full report of her arrival, stating that "her beautiful appearance and the elegance of her interior accommodation are beyond our powers of description". In addition, her captain received special praise for his willingness to show visitors around the ship. But within a month a competitor had appeared. The Liverpool & North Wales Steam Packet Company introduced the *Prince Llewelyn* on the route, boasting that it was "fitted up in the most elegant style with no expense spared for the comfort of passengers". This started a period of intense rivalry between the two companies, each claiming superior speeds, lower fares and greater safety. In 1823 the owners of the *Albion* launched the *Druid* in order to give an additional service, only to be outdone the following year by the opposition, who brought in the *St David*.

The vessels themselves were wooden paddle-steamers, ranging from 150 to 200 tons, equipped with engines of 60 to 70 horse-power, and rigged to carry sail as well. In good conditions the voyage from Liverpool to Bangor was made in about 5 hours, but in rough weather it could take as long as 7 hours. The advertised fares were 10 shillings for a cabin and 5 shillings on deck. These, of course, were expensive, the first-class fare being equivalent to a week's wages for a labouring man. Horses were charged a guinea and carriages 10/6d per wheel. Breakfast and dinner were available on board "at moderate charges", as well as wines and spirits "of the best quality". Some of the vessels even boasted a band. In *Journal of a Governess* Miss Weeton describes her experiences aboard the *Prince Llewelyn* on a passage to Bangor in 1925, made "amidst the noise of steam and steam-engine paddles, double drum, clarionet, fiddle and French-horn". Sailings were made three times a week in each direction during the summer months, but with four vessels operating this amounted to a daily service. The usual stopping-places were Hoylake, Orme's Head and Beaumaris, but in the interests of speed some sailings were made direct to the terminus at Bangor Ferry. The new passenger service proved a great boon to those travelling between Liverpool and North Wales as it enabled them to avoid a perilous land journey, and in less than half the time taken by stage-coach. There was one difficulty, however — that of landing and embarking fashionably-dressed passengers before the building of piers in late Victorian times. The method adopted was to transfer them to and from small boats, but it must have been a hazardous operation in rough seas.

By 1830 the Liverpool & North Wales Steam Packet Company had been taken over by the St George Steam Packet Company, whose greater resources enabled it to put more vessels on the North Wales service. The *Ormrod, Satellite* and *Snowdon* were all added to the Company's fleet during the 1830s, so it would appear that business was booming. These were, of course, in addition to *St David* and *Prince Llewelyn.* Other shipowners, anxious to take advantage of the growing excursion trade, also entered the scene with the *Magdalena* and the *Zephyr,* both of which plied between Liverpool and Caernarvon three times a week. A service was also established from Caernarvon to Bangor, where the *Paul Pry* met the Liverpool packets each day. Fares were 1/6d first-class and a shilling second-class, with refreshments of all kinds available on board.

By 1829 the terminus of the Bagillt route had been moved to Rhyl, and two new vessels were placed there for a daily service to Liverpool. The *Gulliver* and the *Hercules* were both paddlers of 150 tons with increased engine-power "to make the passage even in hard blowing weather". The following year two more ships were added to the Rhyl service, *St Wenefrede* and the *Vale of Clwyd*, and when tides permitted they sailed up the river to Rhuddlan. Allowing for scheduled stops at Hoylake and Mostyn Quay, where a landing stage had recently been built, the voyage to and from Liverpool took four hours.

The excursion service to North Wales was now firmly established throughout the year but sadly, in the summer of 1831, an appalling tragedy occurred which called into question the safety of the steamers. On the 12th July of that year the *North Wales Chronicle* announced that the *Rothsay Castle* was scheduled to sail from Liverpool to the Menai Straits on Monday, Wednesday and Friday mornings, and would return on alternate days. A wooden paddler of 200 tons and 70 horse-power engines, she was described in the press as being "superbly fitted up for the accommodation and comfort of passengers; and from her easy drift of water she is enabled to go close in shore, thereby insuring a smooth passage and an opportunity of viewing the beautiful scenery along the Welsh coast. Her speed is unequalled, the average length of her passage having been only five hours". Despite this glowing description the *Rothsay Castle* was not a new ship. She had been built on the Clyde in 1816 and purchased by a Mr Edward Watson, a shipowner of Liverpool. From contemporary accounts it would appear that the vessel was in a bad state of repair and was considered by a former member of her crew to be unseaworthy. Nevertheless, she set sail from the Pier Head about noon on the 17th August with over a hundred passengers on board. Before she had reached the mouth of the Mersey the wind had freshened, and by the time she had reached the "Floating Light" some 15 miles from Liverpool she found herself in heavy seas. Those passengers who were not already prostrate with sea-sickness begged the captain to return to Liverpool, but either through drunkenness or ignorance of the oncoming danger he stubbornly refused. It took ten hours to reach the Great Orme, a distance of only 36 miles, by which time darkness had fallen and the vessel began to take in water. But worse was to follow. As the storm increased in intensity the cabins flooded, the engines failed and the paddles stopped. With no signalling equipment on board, and drifting helplessly into the Menai Staits, she struck the Dutchman's Bank. The impact caused her tall funnel to collapse and the paddle-boxes to break. Parts of the superstructure were swept away and by two o'clock in the morning the *Rothsay Castle* had completely broken up. Of the 130 or so passengers and crew on board only 21 survived.

The publicity given to the disaster, particularly regarding the blame attached to the proprietor and the captain, at least made other shipowners more safety conscious. A passenger who later sailed on the *Prince Llewelyn* remarked that he found "two signal-guns planted on the poop, rockets secured in the cabin and two excellent boats, completely furnished for service, ready for lowering into the water at a moment's notice". These improvements helped to restore public confidence in the steam packets and inspired passengers to venture further afield. The *Prince Llewelyn* made occasional forays from Menai Bridge to the Isle of Man for a cabin fare of 15 shillings and a deck fare of 10 shillings return.

In 1843 the City of Dublin Steam Packet Company took over the passenger and cargo business from the St George Steam Packet Company, and immediately placed its new steamer *Erin-go-Bragh* on the service. Built at Liverpool in 1840 and equipped with engines of 100 horse-power she was the first iron paddler to be used on the Welsh route. The *Erin-go-Bragh* was followed three years later by three more iron steamers, the *Prince of Wales*, the *Albert* and a second vessel named *Cambria*. Every effort was being made to attract custom and in 1849 the Company acquired a small iron paddler, the *Fairy*, to develop short excursion cruises around Anglesey, calling at Holyhead to visit the construction of the breakwater. She also made trips from Llandudno to the Menai Straits and Bardsey Island, where "passengers will enjoy a view of the most romantic scenery that can possibly be presented to the eye". From press reports of the day these excursions appeared to be well-patronised throughout the summer months. The most well-known steamer in the Company's Welsh fleet, apart from the *Prince of Wales*, was the *Prince Arthur*. Built on the Thames in 1851 she was first placed on the Holyhead to Dublin run but later transferred to the North Wales excursion service, where she sailed on alternate days with the *Prince of Wales*.

There seems little doubt that the resorts of North Wales owed their early development to the popularity of the excursion steamers. Middle-class summer visitors, anxious to enjoy the benefits of sea air and a change of scenery from the drab industrial towns of Lancashire, flocked to the Welsh coast. As early as 1830 the steam-packets were bringing a great influx of well-to-do visitors to Beaumaris. A directory of the day described it as "a fashionable watering place, much frequented in the summer season, the baths being neat, comfortable and well conducted", while a tourist guide referred to it as "a favourite bathing-place, the sands being firm and the water clear". In order to cater for its visitors Beaumaris boasted two excellent hotels, the Bull and the Liverpool Arms, as well as a number of dignified lodging-houses on the Green. A third hotel, the Bulkeley Arms, was built in 1831 and the following year the future Queen Victoria, as a child of thirteen, stayed there with her mother until an outbreak of cholera in the town forced her to move to Plas Newydd. Rhyl was little more than an enclosed common at this time, with a few scattered houses in the vicinity of the mouth of the River Clwyd. But steamer proprietors were not slow to see the potential attractions of the place. Owners of the *Vale of Clwyd* steam packet announced excitedly in the local press that "commodious piers, with every accommodation for landing and embarking passengers, have been erected on both sides of the Voryd at Rhyl". At the same time they advertised that "the sea bathing at Rhyl is not equalled by any place on the Lancashire or Welsh Coasts, having excellent warm sea and vapour baths as well as bathing machines on a smooth hard sandy beach extending for several miles. A new and commodious hotel has been opened, affording superior accommodation at moderate charges". Similarly, Llandudno was little more than a village before the steamboats arrived, but with two extensive sandy beaches within three hours sailing time from Liverpool it could not fail. A surveyor on his first visit to Llandudno in 1846 wrote: "What a marvellous place for a health resort". And how right he was. Ten years later, on one of his excursions to North Wales, Hicklin described Llandudno as "a salubrious and picturesque bathing-place" with accommodation for thousands of visitors.

The coming of the railway to North Wales in 1848 helped to popularise the coastal resorts even further, but it also brought competition to the steamer business. The only practical way in which the shipowners could respond was to lower fares, and by the 1860s a return ticket from Liverpool to Llandudno had been reduced to 5 shillings first-class and 3 shillings second-class. But this was not the only problem. There was also increasing rivalry within the shipping fraternity itself as more and more steamers competed for the holiday traffic. Apart from the City of Dublin Company, which had built up a formidable fleet by 1860, there were at least half-a-dozen smaller concerns attempting to run a rival service. The firm of Price & Case, for example, ran a scheduled service from Liverpool to Llandudno and beyond with the *Menai*, the *Druid* and the *Anglesey*. Two former cross-channel ships on the Newhaven-Dieppe route were also placed on the Welsh excursion service by their new owners, Messrs R & D Jones of Liverpool. They were the *Alexandra* and the *Marseilles*, both sizeable steamers. It was not unusual, either, for tugs to be employed on excursion trips at week-ends, combining this with their normal towage work. The Universal Tug Company of W & T Jollife ran the *Lion*, the *Great Western* and the *Great Emperor* in this way during the 1860s, as did the Hercules Steam Tug Company with its *Ayrshire Lassie*, *Hercules* and *Columbus*. Their accommodation was sparse but fares were low so they appealed to those of lesser means. And to add to the confusion there were a number of other companies which ran a freight service from Liverpool to North Wales but whose ships also carried passengers during the summer season. Examples of such firms were the Menai Steam Packet Company, the Anglesey Steam Packet Company, the Liverpool, Caernarvon & Menai Straits Steamship Company, and the Manchester, Liverpool & North Wales Steamship Company, to name but a few. With such a patchwork service it is hardly surprising that the local press was scathing in its criticism of the poor facilities provided for travellers, particularly regarding the cleanliness of the vessels and the general comfort of the passengers. One correspondent remarked that "the only tourist service from Liverpool which is considered thoroughly satisfactory is that of the Isle of Man Steam Packet Company". In an effort to put things right a new company was floated in 1881, with a capital of £30,000, "to provide improved passenger communication between Liverpool and the Welsh Coast as pleasurable as that of the Clyde and American coasting services". This was the Liverpool, Llandudno & Welsh Coast Steamboat Company, and it immediately acquired the City of Dublin Company's North Wales fleet. In addition, it announced that a new vessel was being built in readiness for the 1882 season which "would steam at a rate of 16 to 18 miles an hour and accomplish the run from Liverpool to Llandudno in two hours". This new ship was the *Bonnie Princess*, a smart-looking paddle-steamer 240ft long and registered to carry 620 passengers. But ironically she was beset with problems in her early days and her owners were forced to charter two ships to sail with the *Prince Arthur,* as the *Bonnie Doon* and the *Prince of Wales* had already been sold. The Company, which had started so full of optimism, was finding life difficult and when a powerful competitor entered the scene in 1889 its days were numbered. Fairfield Shipbuilders of Glasgow had two ships returned on a part-exchange basis, and unable to dispose of them, placed them on the North Wales service in the registered name of Richard Barnwell, the firm's managing director. The *Paris* was a former cross-channel ship on the Newhaven-Dieppe route while the *Cobra,* now renamed *St Tudno*, plied between Belfast and the Clyde. After only one season of serious competition the Steamboat Company amalgamated with Barnwell's Fairfield subsidiary to establish the Liverpool & North Wales Steamship Company. The new Company was registered in January 1891 and for the next 70 years its fleet of fine steamers provided untold pleasure for millions of holidaymakers.

Anxious to provide an improved service the new Company sold both the *St Tudno* and the *Prince Arthur*, and replaced them with a brand new paddle-steamer built at the Fairfield yard at a cost of £50,000. She was given the same name as the vessel she superseded, *St Tudno,* but was superior in speed and was more luxurious, with accommodation for 1,061 passengers. Launched in April 1891, she made her debut on the Liverpool to Menai Bridge run the following month, and apart from occasional trips to the Isle of Man and Bardsey Island, she operated on this main line service until 1912. During the 1906 and 1907 seasons she carried an average of 418 passengers on each sailing from Liverpool to Llandudno, with over 1,000 carried on a few occasions. But on Easter Monday, 1907, the *St Tudno* was found to have no fewer than 1,160 people on board, which was 99 more than the number allowed by the ship's certificate. In his defence Captain Williams pleaded that he and his officers had done their utmost to stop the rush of passengers, but he was found guilty and fined £10. The *Snowdon* had been standing by for the purpose of taking the excess passengers but according to the press report they declined to leave. So pleased were her owners with the *St Tudno* that in 1896 they ordered another new ship from Fairfield's to replace the *Bonnie Princess*. She was the *St Elvies*, and although slightly smaller than *St Tudno*, with a passenger capacity of 991, she was just as popular. Her duties consisted mainly of cruises from Liverpool and Llandudno around Anglesey, excursions from Llandudno to the Isle of Man, and relieving both *St Tudno* and *La Marguerite* on their off-days. As she was a very economical ship to run she was kept in service until the end of the 1930 season, when she was sold and broken up at Birkenhead.

One of the few competitors still in business was a family concern trading under the name of the Snowdon Passenger Steamship Company, for whom Laird Bros of Birkenhead had built the *Snowdon* paddle steamer in 1892. The firm appeared to have been relatively successful since its inception, so to avoid any wasteful duplication of services a sensible arrangement was made with the Liverpool & North Wales Steamship Company for the two concerns to amalgamate. The *Snowdon* had been specially built for the excursion business, having a speed of 14 knots and comfortable accommodation for 462 passengers. Her regular sailings were from Llandudno to the Menai Straits and Caernarvon, as well as around Anglesey. Leaving Llandudno at 10.30 in the morning and calling at Beaumaris, Bangor and Menai Bridge, she arrived in Caernarvon at 1 o'clock, where passengers were allowed two hours ashore, before arriving back at 5.30 in the afternoon. Fares for this passage were 5/6d first-class and 4/6d second-class. Occasionally she ventured further afield to Blackpool and the Isle of Man. During the 3-year period from 1905 to 1907 she carried an average of 131 passengers per trip, while on a specially chartered cruise on the 7th July 1906 she had as many as 453 on board. The *Snowdon* maintained her popularity throughout her career on the North Wales service until she was disposed of in 1931.

The year 1904 represents a landmark in the history of the Liverpool excursion business with the acquisition of what was described as "the finest vessel of her type afloat". She was the *La Marguerite*, built in 1894 by the Fairfield Company for service on the Thames. Her owners, Palace Steamers Ltd, used her to inaugurate regular excursion trips from London to Boulogne and Ostende, calling at Margate en route, and returning the same day. The service, however, proved unprofitable so she was sold to the Liverpool & North Wales Steamship Company in 1904. The arrival of the *La Marguerite* on Merseyside aroused a great deal of interest as she was the largest excursion steamer of her time, measuring 341 ft in length and having a gross tonnage of 1,554. She was registered to carry 2,077 passengers, with every facility provided for their comfort. In addition to a full-length promenade deck and an upper deck she had a spacious dining room, lounge and buffet, private cabins and a shop. Her luxurious accommodation and fittings earned her the apt description of "a floating palace". The *La Marguerite* commenced her regular sailing schedule from Liverpool to the Menai Straits on the 21st May, 1904, and she quickly established herself as the most popular steamer in the Company's fleet. Her long association with the holiday traffic endeared her to thousands of Lancashire and Cheshire people, as well as to those in North Wales. She sailed from Liverpool at 10.45 each morning from May to September, calling at Llandudno, Beaumaris, Bangor and Menai Bridge, before arriving home at 7.30 in the evening, a round trip of 98 miles. In her first season she carried 33,459 passengers to Llandudno, with an average of 500 on each trip. During the next three summers this increased to 605 per sailing, with a record number of 1,830 passengers carried on the 14th September, 1907.

The purchase of two more paddle-steamers brought the size of the Company's fleet to six. First was the *Southampton*, acquired in 1907, and renamed *St Elian*. She was a small vessel of 200 tons capable of carrying 272 passengers, and was used until 1914 on short excursions from Llandudno to Rhyl and Rhos-on-Sea. Two years later the *Rhos Trevor* became available, having earlier been run by the Colwyn Bay & Liverpool Steamship Company, and once acquired she was renamed *St Trillo*. Her passenger capacity of 463 made her a useful relief ship, and she remained with her new owners until 1921.

These were the golden years of the Liverpool & North Wales Steamship Company, both in terms of popularity and profitability. The general acceptance of paid holidays and half-day

Saturdays, together with the extension of the 'Wakes' holiday in Lancashire, resulted in more leisure time for the masses. Helped by an increase in real wages and an improvement in living standards, families were now able to visit the seaside, either as day-trippers or for a week's holiday. Outings were also arranged by clubs, societies and Sunday schools, all leading to an upsurge in demand for pleasure cruises from a wider public. Each summer during Edwardian days over 300,000 passengers were carried on the Company's ships. Llandudno was the favourite stopping-place, and on most days during the height of the season well over a thousand holidaymakers landed there from Liverpool. On August Bank Holiday Monday, 1906, for example, no fewer than 2,817 disembarked there, 2,700 of these being from the *St Tudno, St Elvies* and *La Marguerite.* On 20th July 1907 this figure peaked to a staggering 3,181, and did not even include an unknown number of other visitors brought by the Blackpool and Isle of Man steamers, and by the railway. Llandudno had truly become the "playground of Lancashire". Such figures, of course, could never have been achieved without a convenient landing-stage, and it was only during the last quarter of the nineteenth century, when the pier-building mania was at its height, that piers were constructed at Llandudno, Rhyl, Rhos-on-Sea, Beaumaris, Bangor and Menai Bridge.

Long before the closing years of the Edwardian era all serious competition from other companies had virtually been eliminated. There were, however, a number of vessels which periodically made their appearance on the North Wales route, but which made no lasting impact and were generally short-lived. Examples of those which sailed from Liverpool to Llandudno or the Menai Straits were the *Eagle, Arran, Heather Bell, Snowdrop, Normandy* and her sister-ship the *Brittany.* Then there were three vessels which ran short cruises from Rhyl to Rhos-on-Sea and Llandudno at various times up to 1905, the *Fawn,* the *Albion* and the *Ribble Queen.* Of the others, perhaps, the best-known were the three paddle steamers owned by the Colwyn Bay & Liverpool Steamship Company, the *Rhos Colwyn, Rhosneigr* and *Rhos Trevor.* It will be remembered that the latter vessel was sold to the L&NWS Company in 1909 and renamed *St Trillo.* There was still competition from the railway, of course, which offered cheap excursion tickets to the seaside for third-class passengers. But the Steamship Company had accepted this as inevitable and in fact made an "out by steamer return by rail" arrangement with the LNWR, whereby day-trippers could return to Liverpool by train.

At the end of the 1912 season the *St Tudno* was sold to the Hamburg-Amerika Line for use as a tender to their liners at Southampton and the following year a replacement was ordered. The new ship was a turbine steamer by the name of *St Seiriol*, but because of labour troubles she was not delivered until after the outbreak of war in August, 1914. She was immediately requisitioned by the Government, and whilst on minesweeping duties off Harwich on the 25th April, 1918 she was struck by a mine and sank. *St Elvies, St Trillo* and *Snowdon* also served as minesweepers, while the *La Marguerite* was used as a troop carrier between Southampton and the French ports. Fortunately, all four returned undamaged to resume peacetime sailing in 1919. It was somewhat ironic that, having lost the *St Seiriol* to a German mine, the Company's next acquisition in 1922 was a ship built as a minesweeper for the German navy. She became the second vessel to be named *St Elian*, although she actually replaced the *St Trillo*, which had been sold the previous year.

*La Marguerite's* war efforts were beginning to tell, and a series of breakdowns persuaded her owners that she should be replaced. Amid scenes of great emotion, and with 600 passengers on board, she made her farewell voyage to the Menai Straits on Monday, 28th September 1925 before being broken up at Briton Ferry the following month. Having been the pride of the Steamship Company's fleet since 1904 she had carried almost four million passengers and had enjoyed an immense popularity. The *La Marguerite* was replaced in 1926 by the twin screw geared-turbine steamer *St Tudno* (III). Built at the Fairfield yard she had an overall length of 329 ft, a speed of 19 knots and a gross tonnage of 2,326. Certified to carry 2,493 passengers she was one of the largest pleasure-steamers under the British flag. Her accommodation, which was luxuriously furnished, consisted of three dining-rooms with seating for 203 passengers, lounge bars, ladies saloon, cafeteria, private cabins and a barber's shop. She proved a worthy successor to the *La Marguerite*, and at the Company's Annual General Meeting it was disclosed that she had carried more passengers in her first season than her predecessor had done since 1913. Unfortunately, however, *St Tudno* had to cease calling at both Beaumaris and Bangor because of the difficulty of manoeuvring a screw ship alongside the piers, especially when there was an insufficient depth of water. Instead, passengers were put ashore and taken on board by the Bangor steam ferry-boat, *Cynfal*. But the arrangement was not a success and the practice discontinued after the first year.

Following the immense popularity of *St Tudno*, the directors of the Company decided to replace their old coal-burning paddlers by more efficient turbine steamers. The first to be disposed of was *St Elvies*, and by the start of the 1931 season the new *St Seiriol* (II) was ready for service. She was a smaller version of her sister-ship, being 279 ft long and with a gross tonnage of 1,586. Internally she was an almost exact replica of *St Tudno*, except that she was registered to carry 937 fewer passengers. *St Seiriol* ran a weekly excursion from Llandudno to the Isle of Man, and also undertook regular sailing cruises around the Isle of Anglesey, calling at Llandudno and Menai Bridge en route. Leaving Liverpool at 10.15 in the morning and returning 11 hours later, the sea trip was advertised as "The finest one day sail in Great Britain". In addition to these schedules *St Seiriol* was used on the regular Menai Straits service every Friday in place of *St Tudno*.

To complete the Company's fleet a third new steamer was acquired in 1936. She was the *St Silio,* a motor vessel of 314 gross tons and 150 ft in length. Licensed to carry 568 passengers she was specially designed to cater for short sea excursions from Llandudno to the Menai Straits and Amlwch. In 1946, on her return from war service, she was renamed *St Trillo* (II).

The years leading up to the Second World War saw the three steamers carrying over a quarter of a million holidaymakers a year. With higher standards of living and a fortnight's paid holiday, most workers could afford a cheap day ticket. In fact, fares had hardly risen in twenty years. A day return from Liverpool to Llandudno cost 8 shillings first-class and 6 shillings second-class, whilst a half-day ticket was as little as 4 shillings. Children under the age of 14 travelled half fare, while bicycles were charged 2 shillings for a single journey. Contract tickets were also available, a weekly one costing £1.1s, a monthly one £2.10s and a season ticket £4.15s.

Plans were already being made to celebrate the jubilee of the Liverpool & North Wales Steamship Company when war was declared. All sailings ceased immediately and the three steamers were requisitioned by the Admiralty for minesweeping and troop carrying duties. *St Seiriol* played a big part in the evacuation of Dunkirk, making seven perilous voyages there through gunfire and aerial attacks, fortunately without serious damage.

Sailings were resumed in 1946 and continued in popularity for some years until a combination of factors led to financial difficulties. Increased operating costs, successive seasons of unfavourable weather and the rapid growth of family motoring all contributed to the Company's problems. It, therefore, came as no surprise when *St Seiriol* was put up for sale in March 1962. But worse was to follow. At the end of the 1962 season it was announced that the Company had gone into voluntary liquidation, and shortly afterwards *St Tudno* was sold to a firm of Dutch shipbreakers. This, however, was not quite the end of the North Wales pleasure-steamer service. The one remaining ship, *St Trillo*, was sold to Townsend Ferries Ltd and chartered to P & A Campbell Ltd of Bristol, who continued to employ her on short cruises from Llandudno. She was finally withdrawn from service in 1969, thus bringing to a close almost 150 years of maritime history.

The *Cambria*, which was the first paddle-steamer to establish a regular passenger service between Liverpool and North Wales. This was to Bagillt, near Holywell in June 1821. The *Cambria* sailed daily from St George's Dock, Pier Head, at 7am and left Bagillt on the return journey at 12 noon. Although mainly employed on this route she did make occasional forays to the Menai Straits. A drawing by F.C. Thornley from a contemporary print.

DAILY COMMUNICATION

BETWEEN

*Liverpool and all Parts of North Wales.*

ORIGINAL

North Wales Steam Packet.

THE NEW AND *REMARKABLY* FAST-SAILING PACKET

# ALBION,

*John Emerson, R. N. Commander,*

LEAVES Bangor Ferry at *Eight* o'Clock in the morning, every Monday, Thursday, and Saturday, calling at Garth Ferry and Beaumaris, whence she proceeds *direct* to Liverpool, without stopping off any intermediate place, as heretofore.

She sails from Liverpool on the mornings of Sunday, Wednesday, and Friday, at such hours as to afford an opportunity to passengers for Carnarvon, Holyhead, and other distant places *to arrive before dark.*

*North Wales Gazette*
15th August 1822

W.  R.

*STEAM*

**COMMUNICATION**

BETWEEN

Bangor, Beaumaris, & Liverpool.

THE Public are respectfully informed, that the STEAM PACKET

**PRINCE LLEWELYN,**

*Joseph Wright, R. N. Commander,*

WILL leave Bangor Ferry, Bangor, and Beaumaris, on Monday, the First of November, at Nine o'Clock, A. M. FOR THE LAST TIME THIS SEASON,

Due notice will be given when that beautiful and fast-sailing Steam Packet resumes her station on the following season.

☞ Further Particulars may be had on application to Mr. Joseph Wright, near the Menai Bridge; to Mr. N. Treweek, Carnarvon; to John Brown, *Chronicle* Office, Bangor; or at the Office for H. M. War Office Packets, 21, Water-street, Liverpool.

JOHN WATSON, Agent.

Liverpool, Oct. 26, 1830.

*North Wales Chronicle*
28th October 1830

*Journey to Liverpool and Preston*

| | | £ | s | d |
|---|---|---|---|---|
| September 23. | Car to Bangor and driver | .. | 2 | .. |
| | Boat on board the Packet | .. | .. | 3 |
| | Packet to Liverpool | .. | 10 | 6 |
| | Steward | .. | 1 | .. |
| | Expences on board dinner &c | .. | 4 | 6 |
| | Boat shore | .. | .. | 3 |
| | Porter | .. | 1 | .. |
| | Coach to Preston | .. | 5 | .. |
| | Coachman and Guard | .. | 2 | .. |

Extract from a letter of 1828 in which the writer lists his expenses on a journey from Caernarvon to Preston. With no adequate landing stage at Bangor he had to pay 3d to a boatman to convey him to the steam-packet. His fare was 10/6d (first class), a sum equivalent to over £100 by today's standards. Dinner cost 4/6d, plus a substantial tip of a shilling to the steward. It is, perhaps, surprising to find that a small boat was also necessary for disembarking at Liverpool before boarding the coach to Preston.

An artist-drawn postcard of the ill-fated *Rothsay Castle* which was wrecked off Beaumaris in 1831 with the loss of over a hundred lives.

The *Prince of Wales,* a 400-ton iron paddle-steamer built for the City of Dublin Steam Packet Company in 1846. She sailed between Liverpool and Menai Bridge on three days a week. The cabin fare was 6 shillings, reduced to 4 shillings in 1848, and the deck fare 2/6d. She is seen here at the old pier, Menai Bridge, before being broken up in 1883.

THE CITY OF DUBLIN COMPANY'S Splendid and Powerful NEW IRON STEAMER the

**"PRINCE OF WALES,"**

Of 400 Tons Burthen, and 200 Horse power,

W. H. WARREN, R. N., Commander,

*(Built expressly for the Station,)*

Has commenced plying between Menai Bridge, Bangor, Beaumaris, and Liverpool, and will continue for the Summer on the days and hours following—namely:—

From Menai Bridge, MONDAYS, WEDNESDAYS, and FRIDAYS at 10 o'clock morning.

From George's pier-head, Liverpool, TUESDAYS, THURSDAYS and SATURDAYS, 11 o'clock, morning.

Cabin fare .............. 6s.
Steerage do. .............. 2s. 6d.
Children under 12 years, Cabin 3s. Steerage, 1s.6d.

Further particulars may be had on application to Mr. E. W. Timothy, or Messrs. R. and H. Humphreys, Menai Bridge; Mr. John Hughes, Ship-agent, Carnarvon; Mr. Robt. Pritchard, Post-master, Bangor; Mr. T. Byrne, Post-master, Beaumaris; or to Mr. J. K. Rounthwaite, at the Company's Office, 24 Water Street, Liverpool.

Menai Bridge, 20th April, 1846.

*North Wales Chronicle*
28th April 1846

**REDUCTION OF FARES.**

**CABIN, 4s.; DECK, 2s.**

**Liverpool and Menai Bridge.**

THE POWERFUL AND FAST SAILING STEAMER

**CAMBRIA,**

Captain JOHN HUNTER,

Will leave the MENAI BRIDGE on TUESDAYS, THURSDAYS, and SATURDAYS, at 9 Morning, and will leave LIVERPOOL on MONDAYS, WEDNESDAYS, & FRIDAYS, at 11 Morning.

☞ At the Menai Bridge apply to Mr. Robert Humphreys, Jun., at Liverpool to

PRICE & CASE.
16, Exchange Buildings, Liverpool.

On SATURDAY the 12th instant, the CAMBRIA will sail from LIVERPOOL, at a Quarter to Four, Afternoon, for MENAI BRIDGE, and will leave there on MONDAY MORNING, the 14th instant, at a Quarter to Six o'clock, and will continue every alternate Saturday from Liverpool, and every alternate Monday from the Menai Bridge, till further notice.

*Conveyances will leave the Menai Bridge for Carnarvon aad Holyhead on arrival of the Cambria.*

Liverpool, 20th June, 1848.

*North Wales Chronicle*
1st August 1848

*City of Dublin Company's Stores, Menai Bridge.*

All goods are considered as liens, not only for freight and charges due thereon, but for all previously unsatisfied freight and charges due by the consignees to the proprietors of this concern. Disputed weight or measurement, claims for loss, damages, &c. cannot be allowed, unless a written notice of the same be sent to the office on the day of delivery.

Mr. L. Parry . Pentraeth

**TO THE ERIN-GO-BRAGH STEAM PACKET, DR.**

**FOR FREIGHT AND CHARGES AS UNDER:**

1845

| Date. | Goods. | Weight or Measurement. | Rate. | Freight. | Paid on Receipt of Goods. | Liverpool Dues. | Wharfage & Warehouse. | Total Amount of Freight & Charges |
|---|---|---|---|---|---|---|---|---|
| Nov. 29 | 1 Bag Tob. | | | 1 - | | [illegible] | [illegible] | [illegible] |

Consignment note of the City of Dublin Steam Packet Company, 1845, for a bag of tobacco carried from Liverpool to Menai Bridge on the *Erin-go-Bragh* steam-packet. It should be remembered that the early paddle-steamers carried freight as well as passengers. Lewis Parry, the consignee, was a grocer in the village of Pentraeth, Anglesey, and he normally received his supplies from the Liverpool wholesalers in this way.

The *Prince Arthur*, built in 1851 for service between Liverpool and the Menai Straits, sailing on alternate days with her sister-ship, the *Prince of Wales*. She was a paddle-steamer of 400 gross tons, with a length of 199 ft. She was sold for breaking up in 1891.

The officers and crew of the *Prince Arthur* c.1890.

The *Pathfinder* was a paddle-tug, originally named *Pilot Fish.* Her owners, the Liverpool Steam Tug Company, used her to run excursions to Mostyn at week-ends.

The *Enterprise* was another vessel owned by the Liverpool Steam Tug Company, and when not on towing duties she made short sailings to Mostyn. Built in 1885 she had a length of 118 ft and a gross tonnage of 157. She was broken up at Tranmere in 1920.

The *Alexandra*, built in 1863 for the London, Brighton & South Coast Railway as a cross-channel steamer. She was bought by Messrs R & D Jones of Liverpool in 1886 to run an excursion service to Llandudno and Menai Bridge. She was sold in 1892.

An artist-drawn postcard of the *Bonnie Doon*. Built in 1876 for service on the Clyde, she was acquired by the Liverpool, Llandudno & Welsh Coast Steamboat Company in 1881. She proved to be a troublesome ship and was sold after only one season on the North Wales service, being replaced by the *Bonnie Princess*.

The *Bonnie Princess*, a handsome paddle-steamer of 434 gross tons and 240 ft in length. She was built in 1882 for the Liverpool, Llandudno & Welsh Steamboat Company, and was a familiar sight among holidaymakers until replaced by the *St Elvies* in 1896. She was broken up three years later.

The *Normandy* off Liverpool landing stage in 1902 whilst operating on the Llandudno service for her owners, Liverpool & Douglas Steamers Ltd. Along with her sister-ship, *Brittany*, she also ran excursions to the Isle of Man. Both ships were purchased in 1902 from the London, Brighton and South Coast Railway Company for £11,000. They were 231 ft long, capable of 17 knots, with the *Brittany* having a gross tonnage of 579 and the *Normandy* 605. They were sold in 1902 and for the next five years they sailed from Swansea to the Bristol Channel ports before being broken up in 1910.

The *Albion* arriving at Llandudno pier in July 1902. Built in 1866 as *Princess of Wales* for the Loch Lomond service she was later renamed *Albion*. She had a length of 142 ft and a gross tonnage of 137. Whilst on the North Wales station she plied between Rhyl, Rhos-on-Sea and Llandudno, connecting there with the Liverpool steamers. In 1903 she returned to Scotland and was renamed *Shamrock*.

The *Heather Bell* was built in 1871 and saw varied service in Scottish waters and on the South Coast before running daily excursions from Liverpool to Rhyl, Rhos-on-Sea and Llandudno. She is seen here at Bristol, where she worked for two years before being broken up in 1903.

An artist-drawn card of the *Ribble Queen*, a small screw-steamer of 99 gross tons and built at Lytham in 1903 for service between Blackpool, Lytham and Southport. From 1904 to 1905 she sailed regularly between Llandudno, Rhyl and Rhos-on-Sea.

The *Brighton Queen*, launched in 1905 as the *Gwalia*. After service on the Bristol Channel she was sold to the Furness Railway Company in 1910 and renamed *Lady Moyra*, running sea excursions between Southport, Liverpool, Llandudno and Menai Bridge. In 1922 she was sold to P & A Campbell Ltd, and when used on the South Coast she was renamed *Brighton Queen*. She was sunk in the English Channel during the evacuation of Dunkirk in 1940.

The *Snowdrop* was a former Wallasey ferry-boat and was the first non-paddler to be used there. She was sold in 1906 and was placed on the North Wales service by her new owners, running excursion cruises to Caernarvon. This photograph shows her entering the Menai Straits after leaving Caernarvon.

An attractive advertising postcard of the Colwyn Bay & Liverpool Steamship Company, showing the *Rhos Colwyn*. Built in 1899 as the *Tantallon Castle* she had an interesting career with several changes of name. This card was posted at Llandudno on the 25th September 1903, and bears an appropriate message: "This is the boat on which we went down the Straits under the bridges and round the Isle of Anglesey. We started at 11 and got home at 5.30".

The *Fawn* at Rhyl c.1910. She was a small screw-driven vessel built in 1869 and owned by the Rhyl & Vale of Clwyd Steamship Company, which used her on cruises to Liverpool and short trips to Llandudno. She is seen here taking on passengers at Voryd landing stage before calling at Rhyl pier.

In 1889 two paddle-steamers, *Paris* and *Cobra* (renamed *St Tudno*), registered under the name of Richard Barnwell, a subsidiary of Fairfield Shipbuilders of Glasgow, entered service in competition with the Liverpool, Llandudno and Welsh Coast Steamboat Company. After only two seasons, both companies merged to form the Liverpool and North Wales Steamship Company in January 1891. *Paris* returned to ferry duties on the South Coast, and *St Tudno* (I) was sold to the Hamburg-Amerika Line in 1891, reverting back to her original name of *Cobra*. She was 265ft long with a gross tonnage of 1146. This German postcard shows her plying between Hamburg and Heligoland c.1910. She was broken up in 1922.

*St Tudno* (II) was the first steamer built for the Liverpool & North Wales Steamship Company in 1891, and was given the same name as the vessel she replaced. She had a length of 265 ft, a gross tonnage of 794 and a speed of 19 knots. With accommodation for 1,061 passengers she ran from Liverpool to Menai Bridge every day, except Fridays, from May to September. She was sold in 1912 and broken up ten years later.

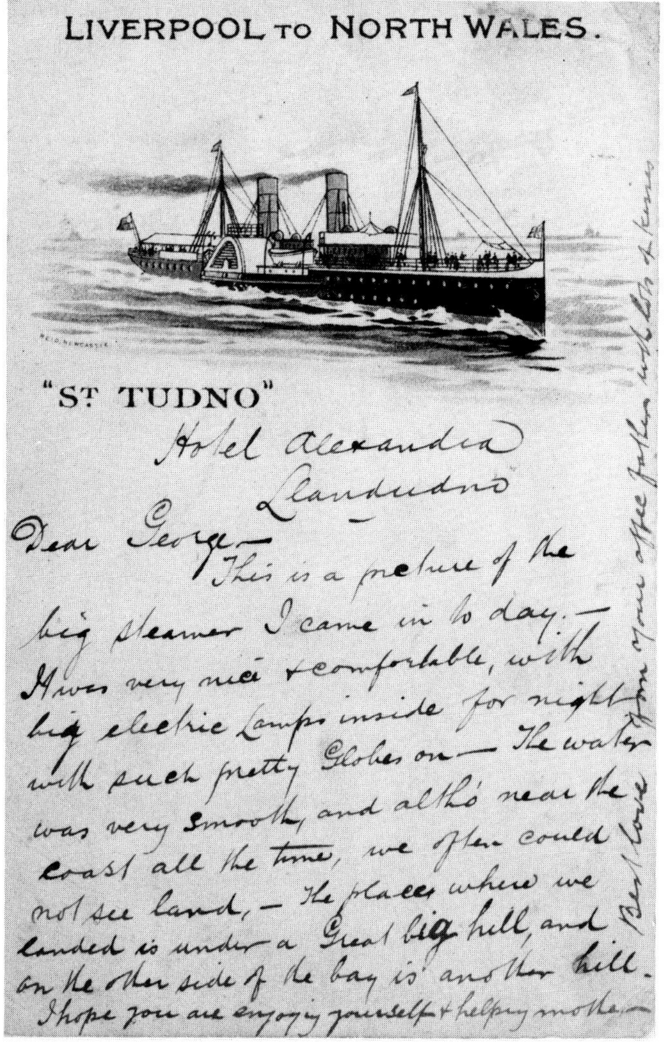
LIVERPOOL TO NORTH WALES.

"ST TUDNO"

Hotel Alexandra
Llandudno

Dear George —
This is a picture of the
big steamer I came in to day. —
It was very nice & comfortable, with
big electric Lamps inside for night
with such pretty Globes on — The water
was very smooth, and altho' near the
coast all the time, we often could
not see land, — The places where we
landed is under a Great big hill, and
on the other side of the bay is another hill.
I hope you are enjoying yourself & helping mother

Best Love from your affec father with lots of kisses

*St Tudno* (II) shown on an attractive undivided back postcard dated the 26th May, 1901, with a relevant message written from Llandudno: "This is a picture of the big steamer I came in today. It was very nice and comfortable with big electric lamps inside for night with such pretty globes on..." (See also cover illustration).

*St Tudno* (II) arriving at Menai Bridge shown on a postcard published by John Wickens of Bangor shortly after the rebuilding of the pier and the construction of the promenade. These were officially opened in 1904 by David Lloyd George, M.P. By 1967 the condition of the pier had deteriorated so badly that it was virtually demolished and replaced by a catwalk down to the pontoon landing-stage.

*St Elvies* seen on her trials on the Clyde in 1896, during which she achieved a speed of 19 knots. She was an attractive paddle-steamer of 567 gross tons, accommodating 991 passengers, and came into service with the Liverpool and North Wales Steamship Company in 1896.

Captain William Williams and officers of the *St Elvies* during her first season, 1896. Capt Williams was formerly master of the *Bonnie Princess* until she was replaced by the *St Elvies*. He later commanded the *St Tudno* (II) and *St Seiriol* (I) during the early part of the war before retiring in 1919.

*St Elvies* leaving Bangor for Menai Bridge on one of her regular excursions around Anglesey in July 1926. She left Liverpool at 9 o'clock in the morning, calling at the various resorts en route, and arriving back at 8.40 in the evening. Breakfasts, dinners, teas and light refreshments were available on board during the cruise.

*St Elvies* leaving Douglas in July 1907 on one of her weekly day-trips from the Menai Straits and Llandudno to the Isle of Man, during which passengers were allowed two-and-a-half hours ashore. The return fare was 9 shillings.

*St Elvies* leaving Liverpool landing stage on her last passenger sailing on Sunday, 14th September 1930. After a career of 35 years she was sold and broken up at Birkenhead.

The *Snowdon* in the Menai Straits in 1926. Built at Laird Bros of Birkenhead in 1892, she was acquired by the Liverpool & North Wales Steamship Company in 1899. She had a length of 175 ft and a gross tonnage of 338. This postcard shows her new, taller funnels which were fitted in 1926. Five years later she was sold and broken up at Port Glasgow.

Captain Highton and officers of the *Snowdon* c.1910. Capt Highton remained with her until 1914 when he took command of *St Elvies*, and was awarded the D.S.C. for gallantry during minesweeping operations with her. After the war he became captain of the *La Marguerite* and of the steamer which succeeded her in 1926, the *St Tudno* (III).

The *Snowdon* at Caernarvon shown on a postcard published by her owners, the Liverpool & North Wales Steamship Company, c.1910. She plied there three times a week during the season, bringing crowds of holidaymakers to this historic town. The two hours allowed ashore gave ample time to visit the magnificent castle built by Edward I at the end of the thirteenth century.

The *Snowdon* arriving at Menai Bridge from Caernarvon shown on a postcard published by the Carbonora Company of Liverpool. Telford's famous suspension-bridge, under which she sailed, is seen in the distance. The postcard is dated the 20th August 1913, and bears the following message: "Glorious sail, very full. Excuse writing, the boat is rocking, very rough and breezy. A lot of folk ill. I survived and all is well".

View of the lounge and buffet of the *Snowdon* on a postcard published by the Pier Studio, Llandudno, 1927. The rest of the steamer's accommodation consisted of a large saloon, bar, cloakroom, bookstall, a ladies room attended by a stewardess and a comfortable cabin for second-class passengers.

# Sea Trips to Caernarvon.

## DELIGHTFUL SEA EXCURSIONS

LLANDUDNO to

## BEAUMARIS, BANGOR, MENAI BRIDGE

AND

# CAERNARVON

A.M. **10-30** MON. †WED. and FRI., 11th, 13th and 15th August. A.M. **10-30**

# "SNOWDON"

Will sail (weather and circumstances permitting)

| *Leaves* | † Wed. only. | Other Days. | *Leaves* | † Wed. only. | Other Days. |
|---|---|---|---|---|---|
| LLANDUDNO ... | 10 30 a.m. | 10 30 a.m. | Caernarvon ... .. | (no call) | *3 0 p.m. |
| Beaumaris ... ... | 11 45 „ | 11 45 „ | Menai Bridge ... | 1 0 p.m. | *3 45 „ |
| Bangor ... .. | 12 0 noon | 12 0 noon | Bangor ... ... | 1 15 „ | *4 0 „ |
| Menai Bridge ... | 12 15 p.m. | 12 15 p.m. | Beaumaris ... ... | 1 30 „ | *4 15 „ |
| *Arrives* | | | *Arrives* | | |
| Caernarvon ... .. | (no call) | 1 0 „ | LLANDUDNO ... | 2 40 „ | 5 30 „ |

*Note—Time leaving may vary. Correct time to be obtained on board Steamer.
† On Wednesday to Menai Bridge, returning at 1-0 p.m., or by "St. Tudno" at 3-45 p.m.

All Tickets are issued, Passengers and Goods carried subject to the Company's Conditions of Carriage, as exhibited at the Company's Offices and on the Steamers.

| FARES (including Pier Dues)— | MENAI STRAITS. RETURN | | CAERNARVON RETURN | |
|---|---|---|---|---|
| | 2nd Class | Saloon. | 2nd Class | Saloon. |
| **Llandudno to Menai Straits and Caernarvon** (Children over 3 and under 14 years half fare). | 3/- | 4/- | 4/6 | 5/6 |

EXCELLENT CATERING ON BOARD.

Sailing bill of the *Snowdon*, August 1930.

*La Marguerite* leaving Liverpool on an invitation sailing to Llandudno and the Menai Straits on the 12th May 1904, prior to commencing regular sailings later in the month. The paddle-box sides are painted black, the colour of her previous owners, but these were later repainted white to conform with the rest of the Liverpool & North Wales Steamship Company's fleet. S.S. *Ivernia* of the Cunard Line is seen in the background.

Crowds embarking on *La Marguerite* for her daily trip to the Menai Straits shown on a postcard produced by her owners and sold on board. It is dated the 15th August 1911 and the message reads: "I am writing this on the *La Marguerite*. We have been to Llandudno for the day. The boat is rocking. I hope I shan't be ill. I am having a very good time".

Crowds awaiting the arrival of *La Marguerite* at Llandudno pier c.1908. Having set sail from Liverpool at 10.45am she arrived in the Welsh resort at 1.00pm, allowing four hours ashore for passengers not continuing to the Menai Straits. Official reports show that on several occasions between 1904 and 1907 over a thousand day-trippers were brought to Llandudno on the *La Marguerite* during the months of July and August.

*La Marguerite* at Beaumaris pier shown on a postcard dated the 13th July 1910. The horse-drawn cab waiting for the arrival of the steamer was one of several ready to take passengers on short tours of the area in the two hours allowed ashore.

Passengers, all of whom appear to be in their Sunday best outfits, disembarking from the *La Marguerite* at Menai Bridge pier c.1905 on a postcard produced by Wright & Company of Bootle. The close-up view of the paddle-box gives some indication of its size. Menai Bridge was a favourite stopping-place for day-trippers, with Telford's famous suspension bridge being a big attraction. In June 1905, for example, an average of 412 passengers landed at the pier each day, 267 of them from the *La Marguerite.*

*La Marguerite* calling at Bangor pier en route to Llandudno in 1908. The pier was completed in 1896 and an average of 34,000 passengers landed there from the Liverpool steamers each year up to 1914. By 1971 its condition had become so dangerous that it was closed to the public but it was carefully restored at a cost of £3 million, obtained largely through grants and gifts, and reopened in 1988.

The crowded promenade deck of *La Marguerite* in 1909, with most of the passengers seemingly enjoying the conversation more than the view. A trip to the seaside was an occasion for wearing one's best clothes, as respectability appeared more important than comfort. The men are seen in their dark suits, starched collars and cloth caps, while the ladies wear their largest bonnets to shelter their faces from the sun.

Captain John Young seen on the bridge of *La Marguerite* in 1910. He joined the Liverpool & North Wales Steamship Company in 1898 and two years later became master of the *St Elvies*. In 1904 he was appointed captain of the *La Marguerite* and he remained with her, including the war years, until his retirement in 1921.

A busy morning scene at Liverpool Landing Stage as passengers make for an already crowded *La Marguerite*.

# AUGUST SAILINGS, 1924.

(SUBJECT TO ALTERATION WITHOUT NOTICE.)

## DAILY (Sundays Included) SAILINGS

From PRINCE'S LANDING STAGE (Weather and other circumstances permitting).

"La Marguerite."
"St. Elvies."

"Snowdon."
"St. Elian." (Twin Screw.)

## "LA MARGUERITE" (Fridays St. Elvies)

| *Leaving* | | Each Day |
|---|---|---|
| LIVERPOOL ... | ... | 10 45 a.m. |
| LLANDUDNO ... | *arr.* | 1 5 p.m. |
| | *dep.* | 1 15 „ |
| BEAUMARIS ... | ... | 2 10 „ |
| BANGOR ... | ... | 2 25 „ |
| *Arriving* | | |
| MENAI BRIDGE | ... | 2 35 „ |

| *Leaving* | | Each Day |
|---|---|---|
| MENAI BRIDGE ... | ... | 3 40 p.m. |
| BANGOR ... | ... | 3 50 „ |
| BEAUMARIS ... | ... | 4 10 „ |
| LLANDUDNO ... | ... | 5 15 „ |
| *Arriving* | | |
| LIVERPOOL ... | ... | 7 30 „ |

COLWYN BAY. Train, Electric Car and Motor Service (week days) between Llandudno and Colwyn Bay in connection with the Liverpool Steamers.

## EXTRA TRIPS by "ST. ELVIES," "SNOWDON" or "ST. ELIAN."

| | | SATURDAYS. |
|---|---|---|
| *Leaves* | | |
| LIVERPOOL .. .. .. .. | | 1 45 p.m. |
| LLANDUDNO .. .. .. | *arr.* | 4 0 „ |
| | *dep.* | 4 5 „ |
| BEAUMARIS .. .. .. .. | | 5 0 „ |
| BANGOR .. .. .. .. .. | | 5 20 „ |
| *Arrives* | | |
| MENAI BRIDGE .. .. .. .. | | 5 30 „ |

| | SATURDAYS. |
|---|---|
| *Leaves* | |
| MENAI BRIDGE .. .. .. .. .. | 8 0 a.m. |
| BANGOR .. .. .. .. .. | 8 15 „ |
| BEAUMARIS .. .. .. .. | 8 30 „ |
| LLANDUDNO .. .. .. . | 9 30 „ |
| *Arrives* | |
| LIVERPOOL .. .. .. .. | 12 30 p.m. |

***AFTERNOON EXCURSIONS, Liverpool and Llandudno.***—Passengers leaving Liverpool in the Afternoon as above, and returning same day, must disembark at Llandudno, and return by Steamer leaving Llandudno at 5-15 p.m., due in Liverpool at 7-30 p.m. **5/- Return** (Saloon). *See Special Bills.*

## *BANK HOLIDAY SAILINGS, Monday, 4th August.*

**8-45** a.m. "St. Elvies" for ROUND THE ISLAND OF ANGLESEY. Anglesey Fare 10/- (Saloon 12/-).

**9-15** a.m. "St. Elian" for LLANDUDNO (Six Hours Ashore). Special Return Fare 6/- (one class).

**10-45** a.m. "La Marguerite" for LLANDUDNO (Four Hours Ashore), BEAUMARIS, BANGOR and MENAI BRIDGE.

Sailing bill of the *La Marguerite*, August 1924.

28th September 1925. *La Marguerite* arriving at Menai Bridge on her farewell voyage, bravely dressed with bunting. There were touching scenes there on her final departure, with cannons and rockets fired in salute. Even the children were given time off school to give her a rousing cheer. Beaumaris also gave her a good send-off, with the town band playing 'Auld Lang Syne', whilst at Llandudno thousands of people joined in singing 'Farewell, my own true love'.

In Loving Memory of

# "Maggie,"

Who sailed her last trip, Sept. 28th, 1925.

---

We sailed upon you "Maggie,"
In sunshine and in rain:
But when you turned our "tummies" up,
We came back in the "train."

Memorial card produced to mourn the loss of the *La Marguerite* after she had made her final trip on the North Wales service. Three weeks later, on the 22nd October, she left the Mersey for the Thomas Ward breaker's yard at Briton Ferry.

# CITY OF LONDON RIFLES

(6th BATTALION LONDON REGIMENT, T.A.).

Hon. Col.: Brig.-Gen. W. F. MILDREN, C.B., C.M.G., D.S.O., T.D.

Lieut.-Col. E. W. HUGHES, D.S.O., M.C., T.D., Commanding.

Presentation of the Ship's Bell

OF

"LA MARGUERITE,"

THURSDAY, 10th MARCH, 1927,

AT

HEADQUARTERS, 57a, FARRINGDON ROAD, E.C.1,

BY

COMMODORE SIR R. WILLIAMS-BULKELEY, Bart., K.C.B.

(Director of The Liverpool & North Wales Steamship Co., Ltd.)

After the *La Marguerite* had been broken up in 1925 her bell was presented to the 6th Battalion London Regiment (City of London Rifles), who were the first troops to be transported by her from Southampton to Le Havre during the First World War. The official programme for the presentation ceremony is illustrated. In all, the *La Marguerite* covered over 52,000 miles during the war and carried some 360,000 troops to France.

*St Elian* (I) off Rhyl pier during her first year of service with the Liverpool & North Wales Steamship Company in 1907. Originally named *Southampton*, she was capable of 12 knots and was ideally suited for short excursion work from Llandudno. She was sold and broken up at Briton Ferry in 1915.

*St Trillo* (I) approaching Llandudno in 1911 shown on a postcard published by G.R. Thompson, the self-styled 'Postcard King' of Llandudno. Built as the *Carisbrooke* in 1876 and later called *Rhos Trevor,* she was renamed *St Trillo* when acquired by the Liverpool & North Wales Steamship Company in 1909. Like *St Elian* she was mainly used on short trips along the North Wales coast.

Captain Williams, officers and crew of the *St Trillo* (I) in 1910 on a postcard published by Pickard of Rhyl.

*St Seiriol* (I) shown on a postcard published by the L & NWS Company in 1914, although she was never used as a pleasure-steamer because of the outbreak of war. She was requisitioned by the Government and whilst on minesweeping duties in the North Sea she was struck by a mine and lost.

*St Elian* (II) in the Mersey c.1925 shown on a postcard published by Cooper of Liverpool. She was originally built as a minesweeper for the German navy but was acquired by the L & NWS Company in 1922 for excursions to Bardsey Island, Holyhead and the Menai Straits, with occasional trips to Blackpool. She was certified to carry 528 passengers and had a speed of 15 knots. She was sold in 1927.

*St Tudno* (III) at Princes Landing Stage, Liverpool, just before embarking on her maiden excursion trip to Llandudno and Menai Bridge on Saturday, the 22nd May 1926, with hundreds of passengers abroad. She was given a good send-off by a large crowd of spectators, and shipping in the Mersey greeted her with their sirens. She sailed at 10.45 in the morning and arrived back at 7.40 in the evening.

# LIVERPOOL & NORTH WALES

## JULY & AUGUST SAILINGS, 1927.

(SUBJECT TO ALTERATION WITHOUT NOTICE).

## DAILY (Sundays included) SAILINGS

From PRINCES LANDING STAGE (Weather and other circumstances permitting)

"St. Tudno."
(New Turbine Steamer)

"St. Elvies."

"Snowdon."

"St. Elian."
(Twin Screw).

THE NEW TURBINE SALOON STEAMER

## "ST. TUDNO" (FRIDAYS 'St. Elvies')

WILL SAIL DAILY FOR SEASON.

| *Leaving* | | | St. Tudno | (a) FRIDAYS, St. Elvies |
|---|---|---|---|---|
| | | | a.m. | a.m. |
| LIVERPOOL ... | | Each day | 10 45 | 10 45 |
| | | | p.m. | p.m. |
| LLANDUDNO | arr. | .. | 1 5 | 1 5 |
| | dep. | .. | 1 10 | 1 10 |
| BEAUMARIS ... | | .. | †No call | 2 10 |
| BANGOR ... | | .. | †No call | 2 25 |
| MENAI BRIDGE (*arr.*) | | .. | 2 30 | 2 35 |

| *Leaving* | | St. Tudno | (a) FRIDAYS, St. Elvies |
|---|---|---|---|
| | | p.m. | p.m. |
| MENAI BRIDGE | Each Day | 3 45 | 3 45 |
| BANGOR ... | " | †No call | 3 55 |
| BEAUMARIS ... | " | †No call | 4 15 |
| LLANDUDNO ... | " | 5 15 | 5 15 |
| *Arriving* | | | |
| LIVERPOOL ... | " | 7 30 | 7 30 |

† N.B.—Until further notice "St. Tudno" Sailings are only between Liverpool, Llandudno and Menai Bridge. Bangor and Beaumaris passengers with single or period tickets proceed from Menai Bridge (free Bus conveyance).

(a) FRIDAY SAILINGS BY "ST. ELVIES" calling at BEAUMARIS and BANGOR each direction.

### EXTRA SAILINGS, SATURDAYS.

P.M. 1-45

Extra Sailings at 1-45 p.m. for Llandudno, Beaumaris, Bangor and Menai Bridge.

MORNING BOAT TO LIVERPOOL (SATURDAYS), leaving Menai Bridge 8-0 a.m., Bangor 8-15 a.m., Beaumaris 8-30 a.m., and Llandudno 9-30 a.m., due Liverpool about 12-30 p.m.

For additional Sailings to and from Liverpool (see Special Bills).

P.M. 1-45

***AFTERNOON EXCURSIONS, Liverpool and Llandudno.***—Passengers leaving Liverpool in the Afternoon as above, and returning same day, must disembark at Llandudno, and return by Steamer leaving Llandudno at 5-15 p.m., due in Liverpool at 7-30 p.m. (or later Steamer as advertised).

**Half Day Return 5/-** (Saloon).

Sailing bill of the *St Tudno* (III) for July and August, 1927.

The upper deck of *St Tudno* (III), looking forward on the port side, on a postcard published by Cooper of Liverpool c.1930. The notice on the right reads: "Passengers forward of this barrier pay first-class fare". After *St Tudno's* return from war service in 1946 the distinction between first and second-class was removed, and she became a one-class ship.

*St Tudno* (III) on the Mersey just before the outbreak of war in 1939. She was a fine-looking ship and a great favourite among the travelling public. Her last excursion trip was on Sunday, 16th September 1962 before being sold for breaking up the following March.

The steam ferry-boat *Cynfal* which plied between Bangor and Beaumaris. In 1926 she was used to transfer passengers to and from the new *St Tudno* at Bangor and Beaumaris, but the experiment was not popular among the travelling public and was discontinued after one season. The *Cynfal* is seen here in the Menai Straits on a postcard published by Cooper of Liverpool.

*St Seiriol* (II) passing under the Menai Suspension Bridge on one of her regular cruises around Anglesey. Entertainment was provided for passengers, including lotto (or bingo as it is known today), an ankle competition and a sweepstake on the time taken to pass South Stack Lighthouse, Holyhead. The postcard has a Llandudno postmark dated the 9th July 1935, with an appropriate message written on board.

Sailing bill of the 'Round Anglesey' sea trip by *St Seiriol* (II), 1935.

*St Seiriol* (II) at Liverpool Landing Stage shown on a postcard of 1939.

The dining-saloon of *St Seiriol* (II), 1939, with the tables set for lunch. Printed menu cards were provided, while serviettes bearing the name and houseflag of the North Wales Steamship Company can be seen clearly on the tables. A five-course luncheon cost 3 shillings and a high tea 2 shillings. Snacks were also available in the cafeteria, where one could buy a cup of tea or coffee for 3d.

*St Seiriol* (II) making her way to Llandudno after the resumption of sailing in 1946, when she became a one-class ship. She was almost identical in appearance to *St Tudno*, except in size and having only four lifeboats on the promenade deck instead of six. Having made her debut on the North Wales service in 1931 she made her last trip on the 6th September, 1961 before being broken up at Ghent.

THE LIVERPOOL & NORTH WALES STEAMSHIP COMPANY LTD.

Telegrams: "ST. TUDNO, LIVERPOOL 3" 40 CHAPEL STREET, LIVERPOOL, 3. Telephone: CENtral 1653-1654.

# DAILY SAILINGS

(SUBJECT TO ALTERATION WITHOUT NOTICE)

## Liverpool to Llandudno & Menai Bridge

SUNDAYS INCLUDED

**From Saturday, 23rd May to Monday, 21st Sept., 1953**

From PRINCES LANDING STAGE, LIVERPOOL (weather and other circumstances permitting.)

"ST. TUDNO" OR "ST. SEIRIOL"

| Leaving | | Each Day | Leaving | | Each Day |
|---|---|---|---|---|---|
| LIVERPOOL ... | ... | 10 45 a.m. | MENAI BRIDGE | ... | 3 45 p.m. |
| LLANDUDNO | due | 1 05 p.m. | LLANDUDNO | due | 5 0 ,, |
| | dep. | 1 15 ,, | | dep. | 5 15 ,, |
| MENAI BRIDGE | due | 2 40 ,, | LIVERPOOL ... | due | 7 40 ,, |

N.B.—Passengers for Bangor, Caernarvon, Beaumaris, and other Anglesey Resorts—Crosville Bus Service from Menai Bridge.

**INTERCHANGE BOAT AND RAIL ARRANGEMENTS** (BANK HOLIDAYS EXCEPTED)

Passengers holding Period Steamer Tickets have the option of returning by Rail on surrendering the Return Half Boat Ticket and on payment of the undermentioned rates, receiving single ticket to destination.

From LLANDUDNO 5/6 From MENAI BRIDGE or BANGOR 6/-

Rail passengers can return by steamer on payment of same supplementary charges at the Steamship Booking Offices, Pier Gates, Llandudno or Menai Bridge.

## HALF-DAY SAILINGS TO LLANDUDNO

These tickets are not available to return by rail under inter-change arrangements.

SUNDAYS 7th 14th 21st 28th June, and 26th July to 23rd August

WEDNESDAYS 10th 17th and 24th June

THURSDAYS commencing 2nd July to 27th August

SATURDAYS commencing 6th June (except 13th June) to 29th August

(ALL ABOVE ALLOWING TWO HOURS ASHORE)

Return Fare **6/6**

MONDAYS commencing 8th June (except 3rd August)

(Return by St. Tudno at 5.15 p.m.)

| Leaving | "ST. SEIRIOL" | Leaving | "ST. TUDNO" each day | "ST. SEIRIOL" Sundays, Wednesdays Thursdays & Saturdays |
|---|---|---|---|---|
| LIVERPOOL ... | ... 2.0 p.m. | LLANDUDNO | ... 5.15 p.m. | 6.30 p.m. |
| Due LLANDUDNO | ...4.30 p.m. | Due LIVERPOOL | ... 7.40 p.m. | 9.0 p.m. |

PARTIES SPECIALLY CATERED FOR AT REDUCED FARES IF PREVIOUSLY ARRANGED (FRIDAYS EXCEPTED)

PRIVATE CABINS may be booked in advance. CATERING, Lunch and Teas, Buffets and Refreshment Bars.

Sailing bill for the daily excursions of *St Tudno* and *St Seiriol,* 1953.

*St Silio* on trials on the Clyde, 15th April 1936, when she made a speed of almost 14 knots. Her maiden voyage to North Wales was undertaken on the 27th May. Unlike her sister-ships she had two funnels, and although smaller in size her passenger accommodation was large and comfortable.

*St Silio* at Amlwch on the 5th August 1936, a popular stopping-place on the pleasure cruise from Llandudno. The small harbour had been used extensively for the shipment of copper from the nearby Parys Mines since the last quarter of the eighteenth century until the decline of the industry a hundred years or so later.

*St Silio* approaching Llandudno in August, 1939, a few weeks before the outbreak of war.

ST. TRILLO IN MENAI STRAITS

When *St Silio* returned to Liverpool after war service in 1945 she was renamed *St Trillo*, thus becoming the second ship of that name to run on the North Wales service. She is seen here entering the Menai Straits, with Penmaenmawr mountain in the background. Her last trip under the flag of the Liverpool & North Wales Steamship Company was on the 16th September 1962.

The *Lady Orme* at Llandudno in June 1935. Built in 1888 as the *Fusilier* she operated in Scottish waters until acquired in 1935 by the Cambrian Shipping Company for service between Llandudno and the Menai Straits, and renamed *Lady Orme*. She was a fine-looking paddle-steamer with a length of 202 ft, a gross tonnage of 252 and a speed of 15 knots. In 1938 her name was changed to *Crestawave* and the following year she was broken up.

For over 40 years the *Clio* was a familiar sight to holidaymakers sailing on the Menai Straits. This black and white former corvette was an industrial training ship for 250 boys between the ages of 11 and 15. She is seen on this postcard at her moorings opposite Bangor pier in 1910, where she remained until being broken up in 1920.

Another attraction for passengers on the Menai Straits excursions was H.M.S. *Conway.* Originally named *Nile,* this former battleship became a training ship in the River Mersey in 1876. She remained there until 1941 when the blitz on Merseyside forced her owners to move her to a safe anchorage in the Menai Straits. She is seen here in 1948 with *St Trillo* passing. In 1953, whilst being towed to Cammell Laird's for a refit, she ran aground in the Straits and was declared a total loss.

POSTED ON
" LA MARGUERITE "

**'POSTED ON BOARD' CACHETS**

Passengers on the pleasure-steamers frequently sent picture postcards to friends and relatives, and these could be purchased on most of the vessels. Many of the cards were written on board during the voyage and posted in the letter-box provided before being taken ashore by the purser and put into the nearest post office. Occasionally, a 'Posted on board' cachet was applied to the card, but such is their scarcity that one wonders whether they were stamped only on special request to the purser. Cachets of various types have been seen from four steamers, *La Marguerite, St Elvies, St Tudno* and *Snowdon*. Some of these are of extreme rarity and less than half-a-dozen examples have been recorded.

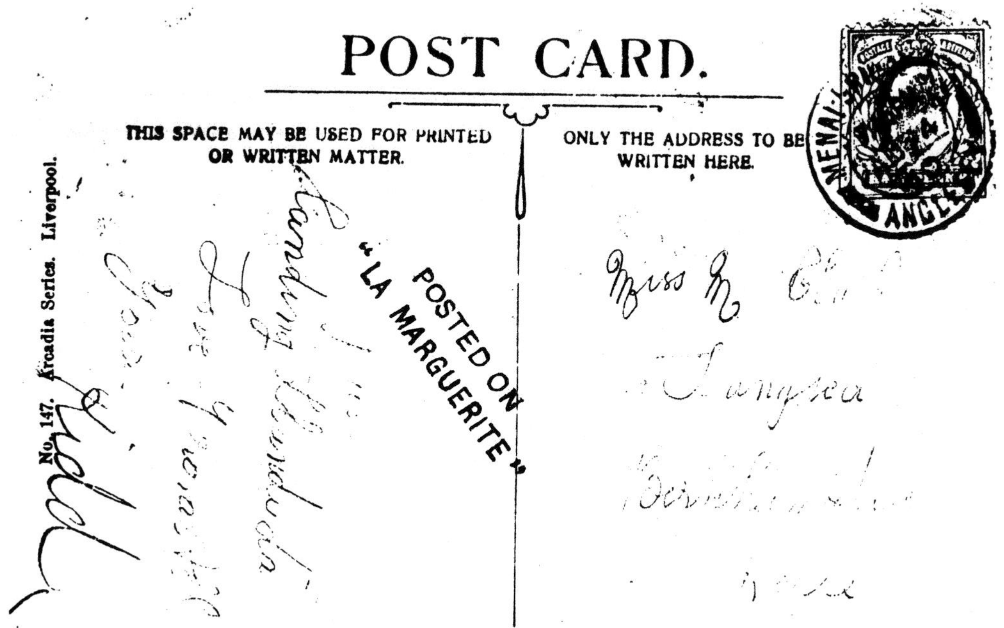


There were two types of "Posted on *La Marguerite*" cachets — a straight line type as applied on this card and a circular one. Examples have been recorded from 1907 to 1914 only, so it would appear that the stamp was lost during *La Marguerite's* wartime activities. Although the message on the card reads "Just landing Landudno", the mail was not put ashore until the steamer reached Menai Bridge, where the postmark of the 4th August 1910 was applied.

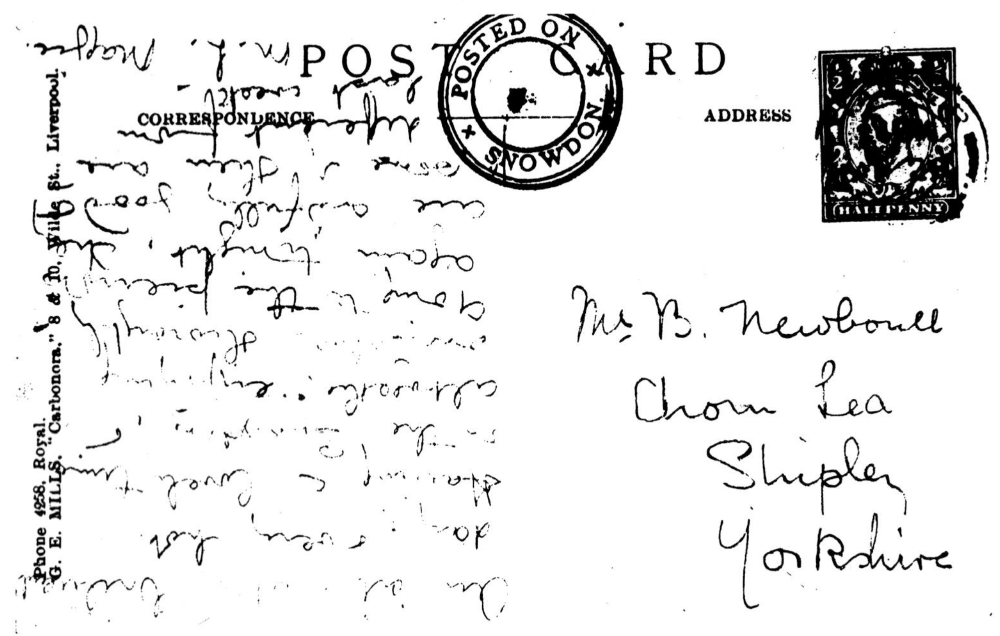


Picture postcard showing a fine example of the "Posted on *Snowdon*" cachet applied in purple, with the appropriate message "Having a lovely time on the *Snowdon*". This cachet had a very short life, having been recorded for the period 1911 to 1913 only. The ship's mail was put ashore at Bangor, as indicated by the postmark of the 20th August, 1913. The postcard, which shows a photographic view of the *Snowdon*, was published by the Carbonora Company of Liverpool.

# BIBLIOGRAPHY

Anthony, H, *Menai Bridge and its Council* (1975)
Davies, H.R., *The Conway and Menai Ferries* (2nd Ed 1966)
Dodd, A.H., *The Industrial Revolution in North Wales* (1951)
Duckworth, C.D.L. & Langmuir, G.E., *West Coast Steamers* (3rd Ed 1966)
Eames, Aled, *Ships and Seamen of Anglesey* (1973)
Jones, Ivor Wynne, *Llandudno — Queen of the Welsh Resorts* (1975)
Jones, P. Ellis, *Bangor 1883-1983. A Study in Municipal Government* (1986)
Skidmore, Ian, *Bangor Pier 1896-1988* (1988)
Thornley, F.C., *Steamers of North Wales* (2nd Ed 1962)

**Newspapers and Directories**

*North Wales Gazette* 1821-27
*North Wales Chronicle* 1827 ff
*Cassey's Directory of Chester & North Wales,* 1876
*Pigot's National & Commercial Directory,* 1828-9, 1835, 1844
*Robson's Commercial Directory,* 1838, 1841
*Slater's National Commercial Directory,* 1844, 1850, 1856, 1858, 1868, 1880, 1895
*Worrall's Directory of North Wales,* 1871, 1874